FOR THE LOVE OF CATS

A Modern Cat Lady's Journey into Cat
Parenthood and Entrepreneurship

MELISSA MEZZALIRA

Contents

To my adored feline babies, Maya and Baby

Introduction

I honestly think cat-loving is just a trait that some of us have inside of us, some lucky tweak of our DNA that gives us a true appreciation for the feline species. We who have this attribute thrill every time we hear a cat meow. Each time we see a cat, our fingers itch to sweep a line from her soft head down to her twitching tail. And the purring... oh, well. The purring fills our hearts with pure joy.

My love affair with cats began at a very young age when I was only four or five. At the time, my family and I were living in Montebelluna, Italy (more on this later), when a little orphan kitten began to visit us. He must have escaped from his home —we never really knew what happened. Anyway, we acted as this furry baby's guardian for a little while. Despite the fact that the kitten was pretty attached to one of my sisters and not to me, I knew right then and there that I absolutely loved cats.

This book is for us cat parents on a quest to understand why we love our felines so much. What is it about the essence of these magnificent creatures that captivates us to the point that we become irrational and will do anything for them? I will also discuss the emerging Modern Cat Lady movement and the social shift from "cat owner" to "cat parent." But, most importantly, I will share my story with you and describe what I've learned through my journey, from Italy to the USA, about caring for our furry babies in the best possible way. My love for cats is so deep that I even chose to start a business, Cats-Essentials, that caters to both cats and their parents.

I hope you'll find some inspiration in this book for your own cat parenthood journey and connect with the feelings of deep adoration we cat parents share for our beloved felines.

The Cat Spell

I feel that my deep connection with these magnificent living beings is somehow hard-wired, heart to heart.

There is an inexplicable love that bonds us to our cats. I call this "the cat spell." For some strange and mysterious reason, these small, fluffy carnivorous mammals draw us to them in a way that other creatures don't. Our love for our kitties goes beyond comprehension and could even be said to defy human reasoning.

Have you ever looked at your furry friend and wondered, *How is it possible that such a small creature can make me feel all of this love?*

If you think about it, we are two different species, don't speak the same language, and don't have the same needs or instincts. Yet, despite all of this, we are fascinated by our cats (even when we don't fully understand them), we adore their wild side, and somehow, we communicate with them through our love.

But what fascinates us is perhaps the fact that cats are their own beings and are not supposed to behave as we want them to. So, we admire (and laugh at) their odd ways to sleep, their zoomies in the middle of the night, and all those other shenanigans that don't make sense to us (even though their antics make complete sense to them).

Although there are some behavioral studies about cats, we as humans are still far from truly understanding the overall cat being. We may not fully understand their essence—but cats captivate us.

I think that cats put a spell on us.

For us cat lovers, we feel an irresistible urge to pet the stray cat, to change our plans to be with our pets and to drop every-thing we are doing to take *just one more* picture of our feline friends.

"Baby schema"

Our obsession with cats has some roots in science. Yes, it's a generally accepted idea that baby animals make us smile. Why else would we share videos and images of adorable kittens and puppies across the Internet? However, our fascination with cats goes much deeper than the fact that they are "cute."

According to a 1943 research paper written by Austrian ethol-ogist Konrad Lorenz, humans are drawn to creatures with small heads, relatively large eyes, and a small nose and mouth. Lorenz called this phenomenon *kindchenschema*, or "baby schema." The gist of this claim is that we are biologically wired to fall in love with infants that need special care for these living things to survive and the species to carry on.

So, yeah, this makes sense. The cuteness of a baby motivates its parents to feed, cuddle, and protect him. However, the exciting thing about Lorenz's assertion is that our connection to our large-headed, big-eyed human babies carries over to all other creatures in the animal kingdom. Cats, dogs, hamsters, rabbits, and all other manners of God's gorgeous four-legged fauna inspire us to fall in love and act as caretakers. Even though we're not from the same species, we are mesmerized by these little beings. Cats even sometimes meow in a way that sounds like a human baby's crying, attracting us all the more.

Small-headed, big-eyed critters attract us and flood our hearts with a deep-rooted urge to love and protect. Add to that the incredibly soft fur that is irresistible to stroke, and we cat lovers… well, we're goners.

Those lucky enough to have a cat in our lives understand the joy that bubbles up in us when our little feline friend rubs her furry head against our legs, arching her back and gazing up at us with wide eyes and that little "W" mouth. This loving gesture is not just cute but scientifically proven to help us bond with our feline friend.

Research has shown that when we pet our cats, oxytocin, also known as "the love hormone," is released in us. This is the same hormone released when people fall in love with other people. According to Harvard Medical School, oxytocin can be released through exercise, while listening to music, and perhaps most notably, when touching other people and animals. When this "love drug" is produced, our happy emotions rise, and we find it easy to bond with others.

When my cats, Maya and Baby, are resting, peacefully purring, on my lap, I can't help but be amazed by the incredible creatures that they are. I feel that my deep connection with these magnificent living beings is somehow hard-wired, heart to heart. If I let my thoughts go for a minute and simply contemplate the sound of my cat's purr, something magical happens. When I rest my hand against the steadiness of their heartbeat, it's almost as if we have become one. I can feel them totally and completely.

My diminutive fur balls are just so perfect. And I wonder: How can such a tiny being be so cute, sweet, adorable, funny, and unpredictable all at the same time? It's almost as if my heart will explode as I take in their irresistible soft paw pads, tiny, kissable foreheads, and small wet noses. My love may seem irrational to some, but I know you, my dear readers, will completely understand how easy it is to fall under the spell of the cat.

The cat spell is timeless

Throughout the ages, cats have put a spell on us. Leonardo da Vinci once said, "Even the smallest feline is a masterpiece." Although we long thought ancient Egyptians were the first culture to revere cats (about 4,000 years ago), a study since then found cat remains buried next to human remains in an ancient burial site in Cyprus that was dated back to 9,500 years ago! Yet another study found a cat's bones several thousand years before in another grave site near the Middle East's Fertile Crescent.

According to Jean-Denis Vigne of the National Museum of Natural History in Paris, cats likely came into our homes and farms with the development of the first agricultural societies about 10,000-12,000 years ago.

"It seems that cats probably came more and more frequently into villages where grain stocks attracted numerous mice," Vigne explained. "I think that humans rapidly understood that they could use cats to reduce the number of mice."

However, the relationship between felines and their ancient Egyptian humans in the Nile Valley went deeper. Not only did cats serve Egyptian households as mice predators and cuddly companions, but they were also thought to be tiny deities who could protect people. Cats were buried in ancient tombs, mummified, right alongside their human friends. Since Egyptians, especially wealthy or powerful ones, used their tombs to represent everything they loved and revered during their time on earth, it is not surprising that their cats could be found curled up beside them, even in the afterlife. Cave depictions of everything they loved in life included pictures of their beloved cats.

Julia Troche, an Egyptologist and assistant professor of history at Missouri State University, tells us that, even though the ancient Egyptians did not necessarily worship all animals, they did indeed love their cats and saw these animals "as representations of divine aspects of their gods."

Maybe this divine aspect or the ultimate sense of mystery surrounding cats is what enthralls us. If cats have been human companions for 12,000 years, that is proof that people have always loved these idyllic animals!

The ancient Romans also revered cats as symbols of independence. However, during the Middle Ages, cats' reputations took a downturn as many believed they were somehow connected to evil powers or witchcraft. Still, this negative image only contributed to the overall magnetism of the feline species. People did not think of cats as mere animals. Instead, they respected these velvety felines as creatures with knowing powers who played a significant role in human society.

Fast forward to more modern times, and we witness famous writers like French author Colette (known for her novel *Gigi*) writing her stories with cats perched near her side. Other cat-loving authors included Margaret Mitchell (author of the epic *Gone With the Wind*), and Beverly Cleary (famous children's author of the *Ramona* series). Another favorite Italian author is Elsa Morante; although childless, she often wrote about mothers and daughters and had an unquenchable love affair with cats. Today, many comic strips, TV shows, and movies feature our favorite fuzzy friends as the stars.

Beyond the cat spell

So, we are enamored with our cats and see them as very mysterious creatures. English humorist and author Terry Pratchett once said, "In ancient times, cats were worshiped as gods; they have not forgotten this."

However, despite the many jokes that cats seem snobbish or aloof, the beautiful thing about our fur babies is that they are not unreachable. If we take some time to pay close attention to their behavior, we can understand a little about what they are thinking and feeling. Every animal has its own essence. As we humans learn to appreciate the core truth of each animal fully, we will substantially deepen our relationship with them.

For example, let's return to the image of a cat weaving its way around our legs. When we get home from work and our cat rubs his head against our legs, he tells us that he loves us.

Furthermore, the cat is leaving his mark on us, covering us with pheromones that he secretes in his saliva and the glands around his head. His mother did the same with him when he was little and returned from his adventures, and now he is doing this with you—marking you as his beloved family member.

In his eyes, you belong to him.

Cats have many other vocal and body language cues that help communicate what they are trying to tell us. They have learned some of these to talk to us humans. For example, they might meow, purr, trill, hiss, or growl, depending on what they are trying to say. We can also assess their mood by watching their stance, ear position, and tail movements. In a later chapter, we'll discuss how to understand our cat's communication.

Research backs up the fact that we can communicate and interact with our cats in mutually beneficial ways. "A relationship between a cat and a human can involve mutual attraction, personality capability, ease of interaction, play, affection, and social support," explains Dorothy Gracey of the University of Vienna. "A human and a cat can mutually develop complex ritualized interactions that show substantial mutual understanding of each other's inclinations and preferences."

In working toward understanding our cats better, we will make them feel respected and loved and encourage them to love and respect us in turn. Our cats essentially see us as larger, non-hostile cats with no fur. Because of this, they talk to us as they would to other cats. So don't be fooled; even though the common myth tells us that cats don't care about anyone but themselves, this is not true. Cats see humans as their family members and want to love and be loved in return.

The more thoroughly we understand what they're saying, the better our relationship with them. Proper understanding encourages solid emotional bonds with our furry babies that will bring us comfort and joy throughout our lives.

2

My Lifelong Infatuation
With Cats

Out of all the pets we had when I was a child, the cats, as you might have guessed, were my favorite.

Ever since that first baby kitten invited himself into our home when I was a little girl, I have been obsessed with the feline species. For me, cat infatuation has been a lifelong affair. I can mark the different periods in my life by the cats that chose me during that time. I had cats as a child living at home with my family. I had cats while away at university. I had cats when I lived in Roma as a young adult. And I now have my beautiful furry children, Maya and Baby, who inspire me to offer the best quality cat furniture I can in my business, CatsEssentials.

My family

I was born into a happy household and a wonderfully close family. My parents were amazing and gave me the best growing-up years a girl could ever have. I grew up alongside two sisters, four and five years older than me. Although I played with them sometimes, the two of them were so close in age that they often spent more time together. I didn't mind that, though. I liked playing on my own.

My little hometown of Montebelluna is in the Treviso province of Italy, which is in the northeast region of Veneto, where Venezia is located. Our town is about a 45-minute drive from Venezia. You might have heard of the Treviso province since it recently became internationally famous for its exclusive Prosecco wine. Treviso is often referred to as "the little Venice" because even though it is inland, it is surrounded by waterways. The many canals and the river Sile give this historical city very picturesque views.

Our area was named a UNESCO world heritage site not long ago to safeguard the cultural landscape of the magical Prosecco Hills of Conegliano and Valdobbiadene and to recognize the exceptional universal value to humanity of the Veneto landscape. It is hard to describe the uniqueness of the landscape and the breathtaking views of those hills. The vineyards perch on steep slopes inaccessible by machinery and require manual labor. The shades of green are very vivid during the late spring and summer months and start to fade at the end of the season when the local winemakers get ready for the *vendemmia* (harvest), usually in September.

In 2009, the E.U. renamed the Prosecco grape with its historical name, Glera, to further protect the term "Prosecco" as a geographically-protected wine. Also, Treviso is the city where the iconic dessert, tiramisù, was first invented! Having left this area at 18 and lived abroad for many years, I have now developed a great appreciation for my homeland. Every time I visit, I remember just how beautiful my part of the world is.

The Triveneto area, which includes Montebelluna, is also known for producing high-quality shoes, leather, and shoe parts, along with other textiles and internationally recognized brands, such as Benetton, Sisley, Diesel, Replay, and Geox. My own family was part of this local economy.

Our family's move—our dream come true

When I was about eight or nine years old, my mom and dad moved our family to a bigger home, to which they built a *calzaturificio*, a workshop attached to the house where they made shoe parts for more prominent brands.

The export-oriented companies supported our local shoemakers, people who were true artisans, creating elegant styles and adhering to high production stands.

I loved this house with its attached workshop—it is where most of my childhood memories were made. Our entire family was thrilled to live in a big house after squeezing into a condo for some years, so we kind of went crazy wanting to have everything we could not have before. We planted a large, beautiful garden in the back of the house with vegetables to eat in the spring and summer, and we added apple trees, peach trees, grapes, and everything in between.

When we decided we wanted a backyard pool, we started digging it—by hand! Every evening and on weekends, the whole family would go out and start back up with our digging, carrying out soil and so many rocks. We used a wheelbarrow and a wooden ramp to cart out all the materials. It was arduous work, but it was worth it and taught us girls the true value of working hard to get what you want. Our family enjoyed that pool so very much over the years.

Cats (and a dog) who joined us in our new home

When my family moved into our bigger home, we began to adopt all kinds of pets. But, unfortunately, that first little orphan kitten who tagged along with us at our condo didn't stay around for long, and we wanted to have some animals in our new life.

In our new property, we had a mama cat who had three little kittens. Back then, we did not routinely spay and neuter our pets, so... guess what? Nature took over! We also had a funny little dog, chickens, and other birds during that time. I suppose we were trying to catch up on all those family experiences we couldn't have had when we lived in the condo.

Out of all the pets we had when I was a child, the cats, as you might have guessed, were my favorite. They were indoor-outdoor cats, but mostly outdoor. After our first mama cat had three babies, the two female kittens grew up and made litters of their own. As a result, we had a bunch of kittens, all born inside my parents' factory.

One of the younger females turned out to not be a very attentive mommy. She would take off for periods of time, leaving her kittens to fend for themselves. What was interesting was that her sister would care for her kittens while she was gone. I believe this kind-hearted mother had six kittens of her own, plus two or three from her truant sister's litter. So that was a load for her, nursing and caring for all of those babies. She became quite skinny, yet she did everything she could to ensure all the babies were okay.

This was a very eye-opening experience for me to see just how amazing nature can be. Cats are wonderful creatures who think beyond themselves to help one another. And each has its own temperament and personality, just like humans do. They are all so different. The one mama apparently had a lust for travel and maybe even a selfish streak that allowed her to leave her babies behind. The other mother cat, however, was sweet and gentle and cared for all of the babies, even those who were not her own.

We ended up finding homes for all of the kittens, keeping only the original three cats that we previously had. I enjoyed these cats so much as a girl, playing with them as often as I could. I worried about them if they did not show up at a specific time or if they stayed away for too long. I cried my little heart out when one of them got lost, run over by a car, or poisoned by something in the industrial area where we lived.

These outside kitties were what started me on my lifelong passion for the feline species. And, after going through the agony of not knowing whether they would show up at night, I decided even as a child that, one day, when I had my own cats, I would keep them indoors with me. So, although my first experience was with these cats, who lived primarily outdoors, I now have indoor cats who genuinely are my babies.

Even though a cat lover obviously loves their cats no matter where they live, I believe an extra attachment develops between you and your kitties if they live in your home with you. You have the chance to observe them in all their daily activities, which allows you to be more in tune with them, better understand their personalities, and have a clear overall view of their health.

For me, this is precisely how it happened: welcoming my cats indoors was an essential factor in my journey from cat lover to cat parent. But I'll get to that distinction in a later chapter.

Even though this is a book about cats, I can't resist telling you about our dog, Remi.

He was the funniest little dog and always getting into trouble. He was permitted to roam freely around the area. And, as I said, no one did much about "fixing" their pets back then. As a result, we had people in the area who suddenly had puppies who looked exactly like Remi. So he was just going around, having fun with all the girl dogs out there.

Remi liked to tease two big German shepherds that protected another factory in town a few blocks away from us. One day, Remi thought the German shepherds were safely locked behind the gate. So, he stood outside the fence, barking and carrying on. However, the gate ended up being partially open. The two big dogs came flying out and attacked him, hurting him pretty badly. Thankfully, after a vet visit and some stitching, Remi was okay, but I think he learned his lesson that day!

Remi also used to chase airplanes, running through the middle of fields and looking up into the sky as though he could catch the aircraft. He was a pretty wild little dog, but his antics were amusing and sweet.

One day, a mysterious thing happened. Remi came into each of our bedrooms in the early morning. He reached up and gave us kisses, wagging his tail all around. Then he left, and he never came back. This was Remi's goodbye. We never figured out what happened to him. We never found him anywhere, not even his body. I genuinely think this dog had another mission in life that he needed to accomplish. His time with us was over—it was time to move on. Of course, I would rather this were true than that he was sick and needed to go off by himself to die. I do believe that animals come into our lives for a purpose. And, when that purpose is accomplished, they move on to the next one. I want to remember him as he was, so sweet and funny and gentle.

Our rescue cat, Micia

One day, my older sister was out walking along a little river not far from our house and found a cat who had been sorely neglected. This poor creature looked like a little piece of white fabric, with shreds of long, white fur hanging from her. She was so thin, and half of her tail was just raw skin. The way she looked simply broke our hearts.

Mamma Rosa, my mother, carefully bathed her, with all of us girls helping out. The poor thing was in horrible shape, and we were so happy that we could save her from the agony of being an uncared-for stray. We named our new pet Micia, an affectionate way to say "female cat" in Italian. Eventually, with us taking care of her, this little cat turned into a very pretty ball of white fluff with beautiful blue eyes.

Unfortunately, Micia was deaf. She couldn't hear a thing. In fact, sometimes, she wouldn't realize how loud she was meow-ing, which was funny. One of us might have been only a couple of feet away from her, but she would meow out loud if she didn't see you—she wouldn't be able to hear you come into the room.

Since she was deaf, we could use the vacuum to groom her, sweeping away the long, loose hair without bothering her with the noise. Removing all that extra hair made her feel better, and the vacuum made it easier for us.

We tried to keep her inside the factory at night since we thought it would be dangerous for her to roam around with her deafness. Despite her challenges, she could live a regular life and be loved. Thankfully, she found us, people willing to see the value in her and care for her. Eventually, she was able to trust humans again. Some mistreated cats just turn out to be wild, wanting to have nothing to do with humans. But not this one. She became a well-loved part of our family.

"There has to be more"—leaving for university

My sisters and I all helped my parents in the family business, supporting them whenever we could. But the two who worked the hardest at the shoe factory were my parents.

After my older sisters left home, I was the last one helping my parents. However, shortly after, when I turned 18 and completed my high school diploma in building design, I decided to attend university, which took me away from my parents and our business. I planned to study sociology.

My motto has always been, "There has to be more." This mentality took me out of my small town and into other places I wanted to explore. I wanted to see more, learn more, and do more. I just never felt that the little town of Montebelluna was where I wanted to be.

While I was away at university, cats snuck back into my life once again. I lived in the historic university village of Urbino, which looks like one of those renaissance villages you see on postcards: a small, walled city surrounded by brilliant green hills and valleys and billowy, white clouds. Urbino is famous for its long history of great thinkers, poets, artists, and writers. It was also home to many prominent figures in the Italian Renaissance, such as Raffaello Sanzio, the world-renowned painter and architect internationally known as "Raphael."

During my second year in Urbino, I shared an apartment with three other girls. They all knew how much I loved cats. So, one evening, one of my roommates showed up at the door and rang the bell. It was a cold winter evening, and she wore a long raincoat. My friend smiled mysteriously as I opened the door and slowly pulled a gorgeous little tuxedo kitten from inside her jacket.

I screamed with joy as soon as I laid eyes on this little fur ball. If only I had a video of this moment of my life—I would have loved to have a record of that perfectly-planned special surprise my friends gave me, along with the emotions I showed when I received it! This was a beautiful gift that my roommates had planned for me together.

Over the time that adorable little kitten lived with us, he brought so much joy into our shared lives. My roommates and I all loved cats. So you can only imagine how spoiled this little feline became, having the undivided attention of four "cat ladies"!

I remember that this kitty was extremely active, even more than most kittens. He used to run and jump around our minuscule apartment. One day, he was running so wildly that he jumped against the balcony window but didn't realize it was closed. As a result, he hit his little nose pretty severely on the glass. We were apprehensive about him as he got immediately quiet—so unusual for him—and sat on the heater next to the sofa for a while. Even though this warm heater was his favorite warm winter spot, he sat there quite a bit longer than usual. Eventually, however, he got up and started flying around the apartment with his usual energy. We were all so relieved!

At some point in his tenure with us, however, this kitten began to go out to the balcony of our apartment and play with the outside cats who lived in the area. For a few days, my roommates and I tried to call him in for food. We could see him running exuberantly down the beautiful green valley behind our apartment building. Even though we called him, this little cat decided not to come inside. He was having so much fun outside with the other cats in the great big outdoors that he seemed to have no desire to come back in with us. After that, he chose to be an outdoor cat instead of living indoors with us. He chose his life. Even though this brought me much sadness, I was okay with his decision and respected it.

As a university town, Urbino was perfect for focusing on studying and making student connections but did not offer much in the way of job opportunities. Well into my third year at university, I had already taken most of the classes I needed to complete my degree. So I decided to move to Bologna. Its central location would allow me to come back to take the university exams, be a little closer to my family, and allow me to find a job. During my five years in Bologna, I worked in retail. I sold clothing, antique frames, and everything else in between—any work I could find that would help me cover my university and living costs. Soon after graduating, my first professional job was in internal communications. After that, I discovered a lifelong passion for e-commerce by working for a leading local company with international reach.

Roma and Mimi

My continued desire to move, learn, and experience new things took me to Roma a few years after I graduated from university, after my time living in Bologna. While I loved working in Bologna, I knew I wanted to move to an even larger city—where better than our capital city of Roma?

As always seemed to happen when I moved, all the details of life fell magically into place. A friend described this phenomenon in my life like one of those children's 3D pop-up books. Turn the page to Roma, and *bam!* There is a whole new colorful page of my life on which to feast my senses. My friend told me, "Everywhere you go, everything falls into place."

I have been fortunate throughout every single one of the chapter changes in my life. Each time I try something new, I feel lucky. I always seem to find a good place to live, amazing people who eventually become friends, and work opportunities that help me grow.

I made the decision to move from Bologna to Roma on an impulse after a summertime visit to a friend of mine, who took me up about a million tiny steps to the top terrace of Castel Sant'Angelo. This massive, cylindrical building was constructed in 135 AD by the Roman Emperor Hadrian as a grand tomb for him and his family. The castle is now a museum, and, during the beautiful Roman summers, it opens some extra areas to the public, like the terrace view and *il passetto*, an elevated passage that connects the castle to Vatican City, an escape route for the Pope in case of danger.

The moment my eyes took in the heart-stopping view of the Tiber River and the Eternal City spreading out below us, the lights of shops and homes twinkling orange against the inky early evening twilight, I knew I was home. As I gazed upon the city, I felt like I couldn't breathe.

"Oh, WOW," I whispered to myself. "*Che Meraviglia!*" Goosebumps rose on my arms. At that moment, I decided I needed to move to Roma. That was it.

A couple of months later, that's exactly what I did.

As I worked to get my bearings in this vibrant, historical, creative city, Lady Fortune revisited me when an acquaintance introduced me to someone who potentially had accommodation for me. This woman would become my best friend. As soon as she opened the door to her apartment, I was instantly captivated by her warm, welcoming smile. Not only did she turn out to be my dearest friend, but she also agreed to share her beautiful apartment—and her cat, Mimi—with me!

Mimi was very sweet and furthered my fascination with felines. He was the epitome of a house panther, with a long and athletic body. He had an inner wisdom that transpired from his eyes and a peaceful essence that you could feel in his presence. This regal cat graciously allowed my best friend and me to live with him in our two-bedroom apartment.

Even though Mimi wasn't technically *my* cat, I loved him very much. Sometimes he would sneak into my room and sleep with me under my covers. It always made me smile because, even though Mimi was trying to be secretive about his comings and goings, I knew that his mom knew exactly where her boy was—and we both thought it was funny and sweet that he would choose my bed. But, ultimately, I knew that Mimi did not *belong* to anyone, *not to my best friend, not to me.* If anything, he saw *us as belonging to him.*

I felt such an overwhelming sense of gratitude to receive Mimi's love. He accepted me wholeheartedly and loved me unconditionally.

Living in Roma was like a dream come true. This city's overwhelming beauty and glorious history are palpable in every corner of the historical center. I was on a mission to discover as much as I possibly could. I wanted to take it all in. One of my most vivid memories is walking down *Il Foro Romano*, imagining the ancient Romans walking on those same cobblestones thousands of years ago. As I gazed at the remains of the old columns, I would try to rebuild the image in my mind of the temple or building that once stood there.

In Roma, I breathed history everywhere I went. The shape of the massive *Colosseo*, always in the background, constantly reminded me of the indelible sign of the Roman Empire's power. Besides seeing my favorite breathtaking view from the Castel Sant'Angelo, I also used to love taking a break at the *Terrazza del Pincio*, a gorgeous terrace that overlooks *Piazza del Popolo*, its view reaching as far as St. Peter's Basilica.

At that time, I was working in a historic office building in the city's center, still in the digital marketing and e-commerce field. What I loved the most about it was riding around the Eternal City on my scooter since it made me feel free and allowed me to discover even more incredible secret corners of the city. For example, I would often stop to take a peek at *I Gatti di Torre Argentina*, an ancient forum also home to many feral cats. It has become the oldest Roman Cat Sanctuary thanks to a long history of caring women—known as "Le Gattare"—and private donations that help keep the cats fed, healthy, and spayed and neutered.

"Almost 20 centuries have passed since then, but Caesar's spirit surely lives on in some of our aristocratic cats that rule over their temples with pride," the Sanctuary's website reads. Although this old *foro* is extremely historical and beautiful, most tourists seem more interested in the cats than the ruins. Isn't that what cats do to us?

I loved Roma very much and was surrounded by good friends. However, eventually, I once again felt the internal call to move on to a different life. When this happened, I had to say goodbye to everything I had in Roma, including my best friend and this darling cat, Mimi, whom I had considered to be my little family.

I had lived in Roma for a few years, soaking up everything the Eternal City had to offer me. But it was time to go.

My move to the Sunshine State and graduate school

I loved living in Roma, but I felt a pull to go somewhere English-speaking where I could take my meager English skills to the next level. I wanted to be able to do more than order a glass of water in English—I wanted to carry on an entire conversation with someone. In Roma, we were always around tourists who spoke English, and I felt frustrated that I couldn't talk with them. Furthermore, I knew that I would never thoroughly learn the language unless I was forced to use it in a real-life setting. Practicing my survival-skill English only once in a while would never take me to the next level of learning. On top of that I was planning to attend graduate school.

I pored over world maps, thinking about where to go. I needed sunshine.

I began considering the United States, and my eye landed on the state of Florida, "The Sunshine State," known for having 360 days of sunshine a year. *Where better for sun?* It seemed like the perfect solution. I love the ocean and the beach—so what was not to love about the idea of moving to Florida?

I used to drive down to the coast and sit on the beach in the evenings, relaxing my mind and taking it all in. I remember looking out across the water, thinking, *On the other side of this water is Florida*. So, armed with my old mantra, "There has to be more," I packed a couple of suitcases and traveled across the ocean to Florida to see what the United States of America was all about.

3

We Are Cat Parents, Not Cat Owners

Cat lovers don't think of their cats as pets. Instead, they are beloved family members.

I just shared the story about the wise and loving Roman cat, Mimi. My friend and I didn't own him—instead, he *allowed* us to be his family. She was his devoted mom, and I became his loving adopted aunt. In my opinion, the relationship between a cat and his human is comparable to the one of a baby with his mama or dad. Many of us cat lovers share the same sentiment: our cats are our babies.

We don't own our cats

If there's one thing I can't accept, it's the term "cat owner." Or, really, the term "pet owner," in general. The recent trend of people defining themselves as "cat mom," "cat daddy," or "cat parent" makes my heart sing since it means more people realize just how deep and meaningful our connection with our furry companions is. They are part of our family and, in some cases, are the only family we have. I pride myself on being a cat mother to my two cat children, Maya and Baby. They are the light of my life and the inspiration behind my business.

I hate the term "cat owner" because it devalues each cat's independence and individuality by making it seem as though they are nothing more than an inanimate possession—just something to own and take care of but not a divine creature in and of itself. For decades, I have cringed whenever I heard this term.

Cats are living, breathing creatures with souls and distinct personalities. When we say we "own" them, we are belittling not only them as sentient beings but also betraying the bond we share with our companions. We're minimizing their role in our lives, providing us with joy, happiness, and love. We, as humans, don't own cats.

It is clear that the shift from "cat owner" to "cat parent" has already begun—thankfully! Let's stop cat ownership and consider our furry companions true family members.

How many is enough?

Just as a girl can never have too many shoes, a cat lover can never have too many cats. Now, I am not promoting cat hoarding here because a big part of being a cat parent is to be responsible for the well-being and happiness of your kitty (or kitties or many kitties). So, it's great to rescue many cats, as long as you can offer them a better life than they would have had in the streets.

Once a person has shared their home with a cat, they often see no reason not to share it with more than one. That's why, when we talk to other cat lovers, our first question is usually, *How many cats do you have?* We don't care what breeds they are or whether they are male or female. No, instead, *the number* of cuddly companions seems to be the first question we ask each other.

Studies have found that more than half of cat parents have at least two cats. But how many should you have? Well, that depends on your ability to take care of them. Cats need more than just food and litter boxes. Even though they are often considered low-maintenance companions, much more ensures they are happy and healthy (more on this in a later chapter). Cats need attention, playtime, enrichment, and of course, cuddles. On top of that, the more cats, the higher the supplies and vet costs will be. So, there is also an economic factor to consider that we sometimes overlook.

Yes, we cat lovers are wired to help them all and are so proud and happy to share our rescue stories. But we also have to consider what we can offer these beautiful souls, an analysis similar to deciding how many kids we want (and how many we can afford to take care of). Once we bring them into our homes, these beautiful kitties become our responsibility, no matter how independent we want to believe they are.

There isn't a magic formula to calculate how many cats we should have. It just depends on your lifestyle, preferences, and the type of environment you're able to provide for your feline family.

Maya and Baby

After all the many cats I've had in my life, when I moved to the United States, I chose to have two cats: Maya and Baby. Or maybe they chose me... who knows? In any case, these two magnificent creatures became my family away from home. On a routine basis, they comfort, support, and inspire me. They are like my little guardian angels.

When I was in the US for about three years, my life in this giant new country finally started to take shape. But, unfortunately, this last move didn't go as smoothly as my previous ones. So when I turned the page of that 3D book that is Melissa's life, the positive events did not pop up as quickly as they usually did! Moving across the ocean to a different country with a new language, new rules and laws, and cultural differences... well, let's just say it wasn't easy. But I am glad I didn't know that things would be a little more difficult for me with my next move, or else I might not have taken the leap!

When I first moved to the US, things were pretty stressful. I wasn't necessarily thinking of inviting cats into my life. But, as always, cats find their way to us. So read on to hear my two rescue stories, Dear Cat Lovers, and how Maya and Baby found their way into my life and my heart.

The first one to find me was Maya. When I discovered this unnerved kitten abandoned and shivering in a public restroom, I knew right then and there that this little girl was meant for me. Something in the divine plan of the Universe sent her to me. The poor girl huddled next to a handwritten sign that offered some paltry information: her name, the fact that she was fixed and vaccinated, and that her person could not take her to New York, where they were moving. This person did not elaborate on why they could not take their cat.

I never want to judge anyone since I don't know a person's full story. However, in my opinion, *you do not, under any circumstances, leave your fur babies behind!* Maya was about six months old, a gorgeous tuxedo cat with Egyptian cat-like features, a graceful, long body, large almond-shaped green eyes, and lean and athletic legs. She was totally frightened and in the depths of despair. I also think she was probably pretty heavily disappointed by the human who had deserted her, feeling that the entire human species had let her down.

Getting close to Maya was difficult due to all the growling and hissing. But, really, who wouldn't hiss and growl during such a traumatic experience? Somehow, I was able to pick her up, avoiding the razor blades of her claws, and get her into a box so that I could take her home.

For the entire first week at my house, she hid behind the TV. I set some food nearby, hoping to offer her the sustenance her skinny little body needed, but she barely ate a morsel. By this point in my life, I'd had quite a lot of experience with cats. Even so, I was anxious that I wouldn't be able to conquer the heart of this one. It seemed to be taking forever for Maya to come out of her terror.

But guess what? A few days later, she started picking her way carefully from behind the TV and eating small bits before scurrying back to her hiding spot. Little by little, she got more courageous and started coming closer and closer to me. When I finally felt she'd reached a small breakthrough and became daring enough, I sat very still and let her approach me. The first time I was able to pet her, a spear of joy bubbled up in me and her both—human woman and feline little girl—and, from that moment on, I worked to gain her precious trust more and more.

At some point, I called a mobile cat groomer because I wanted to make sure she was clean of fleas and any other nastiness she might have acquired in that public bathroom. Maya's first grooming session was actually a pretty funny experience. The groomer parked his van in my building's lot, and I brought Maya, in her carrier, to him downstairs. As I was leaving her in the van with the groomer, I mentioned that my little girl might be a bit aggressive since she had experienced the trauma of abandonment and God knows what else. After returning to my apartment, I watched from the windows to monitor whether the van might be shaking side-to-side from a fight between the hysterical Maya and the poor groomer. I half-expected to see the man come flying out of the van, screaming.

None of that happened. Instead, the groomer called me about 30 minutes later. I held my breath as he started to speak. I need not have worried, though, since he told me that Maya was very calm and collected during the whole grooming session. I was relieved—and quite surprised!—to hear the grooming session had been a success. When I went downstairs to pick her up, Maya looked just beautiful. She smelled sweet and fresh and was pretty with a colorful bandana tied around her long, elegant neck. When I picked her up, she nuzzled against my neck, purring. I knew she was proud of looking and feeling so good.

From that time on, Maya and I became very close. She started to trust me, and the two of us became quite the team. Every night, she slept with me on my pillow. If I stirred, she would purr me back to sleep, protecting her mama from any dangers in the dark house at night. Maya gave me a sense of peace, and I certainly hope I gave her the same feeling of being home, being safe.

After about a year, I decided that perhaps Maya needed a furry companion. By that time, I was working long hours in a luxury retail position, so I thought it would be beneficial for her to have company when I wasn't able to be home with her during the day.

I walked into one of Petco's adoption events one weekend, telling myself that I "just wanted to check it out." I didn't know how these events worked, but as soon as I walked up, a pet foster mom took one look at me and wordlessly handed me a tiny, gray, velvety ball of fur. The kitten immediately fell asleep on my arm. I took that as a sign that I was chosen again by another beautiful feline creature. There was no way in the world I couldn't take him home with me after that. I'd been chosen!

The fluffy ball of velvet was called Smokey, but since he was so young, I felt it would be fine to change his name. He became Baby. To me, he was the "baby" of my family. And, surprise, surprise, this simple name absolutely suits his funny and happy little personality quite well.

Even though I tried to introduce Maya to Baby with care and respect for Maya's seniority in our home, things took much longer than I had hoped for. After all, by now, Maya considered herself to be the house princess. She was not only protective of me but also a bit possessive. When Baby arrived, she made it known, in no uncertain terms, that I was *her* mom, and she was *the boss* of the house.

However, with some time, even my beautiful, aloof princess Maya could not resist Baby's playful charm. Baby was a Russian blue mix with green, spirited eyes and an uncontrollable energy that got him into trouble over and over, much to the amusement of both me and Maya. How many times do the two of us girls watch Baby's antics, shaking our heads at his preposterousness? I swear I've caught Maya rolling her eyes a time or two!

I truly feel that my cats have chosen me. These two magnificent creatures have become my family away from home. But they are more than pets to me; they are my babies, companions, protectors, inspiration for my business, and, as I said above, my tiny, furry guardian angels.

From cat lover to responsible cat parent

I'd promised myself when I was a little girl that, when I had cats as an adult, they would live indoors with me. So Maya and Baby are indoor cats. I want to give them the best and longest life possible, and, in my eyes, this is the best way to do it. Living with Maya and Baby in our house allows me to watch them in all of their daily routines and activities, which helps me know them very deeply. I can better understand their personalities and their likes and dislikes, as well as guess more accurately what they need at any given moment.

My two furry babies have been an incredible journey for my personal and spiritual growth. They make me experience the most beautiful and unconditional love I could ever imagine, and they challenge me daily to be the best cat parent I can be. I am fully responsible for these two gorgeous little beings. Without me, they would not be able to survive indoors independently. Not only am I called to take better care of them, but I have been transformed from simply a cat lover to a responsible cat parent.

Cat lovers vs. dog lovers

According to the American Pet Products Association's 2021-2022 National Pet Owners' Survey, 35% of U.S. households welcome cats into their lives, which means a whopping 45.3 million families have over 95 million cats. The statistics don't lie—cats are every bit a human's best friend as a dog might be.

I've always found it comical how people like to polarize themselves into camps. How often have you been asked, "Are you a cat lover or a dog lover?" Why do we need to choose? Every animal has a distinct personality and is beautiful in its own way. Yes, cats do cat things, and dogs do dog things. Hey, cats don't fetch a ball, but dogs don't purr. But who cares? Why limit your love? There should be no divide between cat and dog lovers; we should simply all celebrate our appreciation for these animals that have chosen to spend their lives with us.

Whatever kind of animal suits your personality type and spirit is absolutely fine. There's no reason to judge each other. For as long as we can remember, dog and cat lovers have done just that, attaching certain personality traits to each other. *Well, if you're a dog lover, you must be an outdoorsy person who is capable, robust, energetic, and outgoing.* On the other hand, cat lovers tend to be homebodies who are more sensitive and introspective. Perhaps these stereotypes evolved from the fact that dogs need to be walked outside, whereas cats can live indoors at all times and also seem to be more independent and cautious. But are these stereotypes accurate?

When people think of "man's best friend," the image that springs to mind is usually the golden retriever, husky, or German shepherd. Rarely do people think of cats first. However, if you ask a cat lover, they'll immediately light up and begin sharing wonderful stories about their beloved Floof (or Chunker or Son or Precious Fluff Angel or… you get the idea). Cat lovers have the utmost affection for their feline companions and know they are lucky to have the chance to wake up and experience the love of these whiskered furry babies in their homes.

Whether they're accurate or not, my argument is that these stereotypes do not matter. For some reason, people like to lump other people into categories. In Chapter Four, I will debunk the myth of the stereotypical "Crazy Cat Lady" and describe the vibe and style of the Modern Cat Lady.

Our babies and our best friends

For those of us who love cats, the cat *is* our best friend. We give them everything they need: food, water, a whole house to explore as though it were a jungle adventure zone, and our affection and respect. We choose to share our home with these intelligent fur balls and, in exchange, they choose to share their lives with us. We love them; they love us back, showing us through their nose boops, purrs, and gentle love nips. We treat them well, and they take good care of us too. They bring us delicious treats like dead mice, leaves, or bumblebees, lick our hands to make sure we're clean, and snuggle up to keep us safe.

Cat lovers don't think of their cats as pets. Instead, they are beloved family members.

4

The Modern Cat Ladies

As cat lovers, we, the modern cat ladies, are confident in our preference to share our lives with one or more cats. We do not pretend to be someone we are not, and we are unapologetically devoted to our furry babies.

It's always interesting for me to share stories with fellow cat lovers in the pet store aisles. I smile when I see someone picking up cat food or litter from the shelves since it makes me feel good to know this other person is taking care of cats too and that a total stranger now has something in common with me—a deep and overwhelming love for cats. Since we typically don't walk our cats, it's sometimes harder to spot a cat parent than a dog parent. However, as soon as I learn that someone loves cats, I feel a connection—here is a kindred spirit with a cat addiction, just like me!

When I meet a fellow cat parent, I know we are both cat-loving, cat-obsessed cat advocates. One thing we are not, however, is "Crazy Cat Ladies."

I detest the "Crazy Cat Lady" stereotype. Where does it even come from? Maybe it's just our human desire to put a label on everything and everyone. Or maybe it comes from the Crazy Cat Lady character on *The Simpsons*, who always has cats hanging from her, blathers gobbledygook, and appears much older than her 40 years.

Debunking the "Crazy Cat Lady" cliche

We, modern cat people, are so much different than this tired, old stereotype, which paints the picture of a single, growing-older-by-the-day lady who talks to herself and is incapable of developing healthy human relationships. In addition, this nutty woman is often thought to be a terrible housekeeper, with the smell of dirty litter boxes wafting from her windows and cat hair covering all the surfaces in her home.

Let's face it. Pigeonholing cat lovers in this way harms both cats and the women who love them. So why not call it what it is: a misogynistic way of judging and insulting women who don't fit into a traditional role? It makes me feel very irritated. This is why I want to debunk the misconception of the "Crazy Cat Lady" once and for all.

First of all, we cat parents are not necessarily all *ladies*. While 58% of Americans who have cats in their households happen to be female, that's only a little more than half of all cat people in the US. Many men have cats or treat the cats who live with them in their homes like family. Should we call these guys "Crazy Cat Gents"? No, because there is nothing crazy about loving a certain kind of animal. I respect and appreciate the men who show devotion and truly "get" our feline friends.

Secondly, many people picture those who love cats as old, single women who are weird, anti-social, and disheveled. This is simply not true. Instead, modern cat ladies can be of any age or relationship status. In addition, we can have any kind of social attitude or personality. The only common ground among people who love cats is we are crazy about our cats! And, in some cases, we may even love them more than we love *people*. That's it. That's the only conclusion we should be drawing. All else would be unfair (and likely untrue) conjecture.

Most modern cat ladies I have met are compassionate people who love animals. They are often as independent as the cats they live with and just as amazingly fascinating as the cats they love. Usually, these women are also intellectually curious, non-conformist, stylish, and have a keen eye for design.

Nothing like the weird, old spinster described in *The Simpsons*, right?

My third point argues that you are not a crazy cat lady if you have more than one cat. Some people simply choose to have more than one pet. It's as simple as that. So whether you are a one-cat household or have opened your door to seven feline friends, you're not crazy—you just think cats are adorable and want to share your love with many of them. Who could blame you?

Last, some people believe that if you love cats, then you're the crazy cat lady who could not possibly love dogs. This, too, is so wrong. Enjoying cats in your life does not preclude you from loving dogs. It simply means that you've chosen to live your best life with felines around—and, in some cases, you might even have a dog or two living in your home as well. Generally speaking, people who love cats are in communion with Mother Nature and love all of the beautiful species she has given to us. I am an example of this myself, loving and respecting all creatures who live on this planet. I've had the privilege of sharing my life with both cats and dogs at the same time. Just because I love cats does not mean I don't also love dogs.

"Although there's a widespread stereotype of cat owners, especially women, as eccentric, chronically single, and distinctively neurotic, researchers found no evidence to support that image," according to a 2019 article by Gabby Landsverk published on Insider.com. "In fact, cat owners were not more likely to self-report depression, anxiety, or interpersonal relationship problems than other groups."

Unapologetically cat-loving

Part of the mission of my business, CatsEssentials, is to crush these catastrophic cat lady stereotypes. So many people are coming forward these days to celebrate cat lovers and cat parents as cool and modern. I think the idea of the "The Modern Cat Lady" is here to stay.

The modern cat lady (or even modern cat gent) is a person who loves and appreciates cats and wants the best for their feline family members. We cat lovers need to know that we can claim our love for our furry friends without being judged by society and shoved into the "weird" box. As cat lovers, we, the modern cat ladies, are confident in our preference to share our lives with one or more cats. We do not pretend to be someone we are not, and we are unapologetically devoted to our furry babies.

It is our own decision which animal we choose to share our life with. If we love the idea of a creature that is independent yet loving and playful while also being the best nap buddy in the world, then, of course, we will choose a cat. If we want to share our lives with an animal that is more knowing than some, who is to tell us differently? If we like the idea that cats are good for our physical health, then cats are for us. And it's true—cats lower our blood pressure and our risk of heart attack. And their loving presence also releases dopamine and serotonin, which help regulate our moods, reduce stress, and improve our immune functioning.

Things we modern cat ladies learn from our cats

Cats are champion nappers, sleeping up to 18-20 hours a day, and make excellent housemates due to their somewhat laid-back nature. As master relaxers, our furry friends remind us to take it easy. In addition, they are playful and childlike and help keep us feeling spontaneous and free. Cats know how to remain in the present moment, something they teach us every time they snuggle on our laps or bring us a toy to play with.

Have you ever noticed how energetic cats can be when they're playing? When they zoom, they *zoom*. Whether chasing, scratching at their favorite post, or running laps around the house, cats are serious about their play. Much like children, they are all in when they are romping around. When you play with them, you remember how to stay lighthearted and keep having fun. That's what life is all about, right?

Cats don't criticize us, even if they seem to be aloof. Instead, they abide by a "live and let live" mentality. Their calm, collected nature reminds us modern cat ladies not to take ourselves too seriously.

In addition, cats love us purely and unconditionally. We should feel blessed to be able to share our lives with our cats and take the time to listen to what they're trying to teach us. Cats usually live relaxed, happy lives, a contented way of being more of us should strive for. Our cats are not only our babies but also wise role models.

These are all well-considered, personal reasons to invite a cat into your life. The modern cat lady knows these things and isn't afraid to make her choice based on her personal preferences and not on what other people might think. We, the modern cat ladies, know the truth—cats are beautiful, magical creatures, and we should consider ourselves lucky to have them in our lives.

5

How I Became A Catpreneur and Started CatsEssentials

I started CatsEssentials because I believe modern cats deserve the best—and modern cat ladies (and gents) deserve to have products for their furry babies that are just as beautiful as both they and their cats are.

When you live and breathe cats every day, and you are as passionate about them as I am, then it's natural that you would be inspired to make their lives better.

Maya and Baby are my inspiration

My mission to improve the lives of not only my cats but cats everywhere started when I began to notice how addicted Baby was to his canned food. I also started noticing that his fluffy belly was getting, shall we say, *puffier*. This started me on a mission to read tons of books and articles about healthier cat food choices. I realized that many canned foods often incorporate low-quality ingredients and could be detrimental to my kitties' health. So I decided I would switch their diet to one that was cleaner and more protein-based. Maya and Baby have been enjoying their healthy, freeze-dried food for some years now, and they seem much more active and healthier.

This closer look into providing the best lives for my babies started a chain reaction for me. I began to look for ways to improve my cat children's existence in all the ways I could. I analyzed everything from the toys I was letting them play with to the cat beds they slept in. I started taking everything apart, looking at how these things were made. I wanted to make sure there were no harmful ingredients in these items I was letting my cats play with, chew on, and sleep in on a daily basis.

Unfortunately, most of us never realize how many toxins and chemicals we have around us in our homes. Many of the items we bring into our houses—even the furniture—are made with harmful materials. I pulled apart nearly all of my cats' belongings, only to find synthetic, toxic materials the manufacturers had used to keep costs low. Synthetic fabrics often are colored with dyes and chemicals that can cause many health issues, including respiratory diseases, allergic reactions, and sensitivities. On top of that, studies have found that flame retardants in furniture might be connected to cat hyperthyroidism.

As I learned about the risks of some of these toxins for my cats' health, I also began to notice, frustrated, that there was quite a lack of pretty, modern-styled furniture available for me to purchase for my babies. Feeling the lack of this, I became inspired to create my own line of furniture that would reflect everything I couldn't find for sale on the market. I wanted furniture that was: 1) aesthetically pleasing, 2) made from quality, natural materials, and 3) created through fine, artisanal craftsmanship.

Maya and Baby were definitely the inspiration behind my new business pursuit. Like any cat parent, I wanted my furry babies to live long and healthy lives. I also wanted to spoil them. They deserved the best cat beds possible. I wanted their beds to be comfortable and customizable to their preferences and also be safe and healthy. I knew deep down that we cat parents want our precious babies—and their beautiful furniture—to be the center of attention in the room!

Putting it all together

As someone born and raised in a family of skilled artisans, I always knew I wanted to have my own business. As a teenager, I watched my parents making quality shoe parts for some pretty big brands. As a result, I absorbed my parents' uncompromised commitment to product excellence from a young age.

I was brought up in an entrepreneurial environment, then went on to learn about building design in my technical school. After that, I graduated with a master's degree in international business from Florida International University. All of these life events helped it become evident to me that I wanted to create my own business. In addition, having grown up surrounded by the beauty of the Prosecco country, the architecture of Venezia, and the history of Roma, I developed a keen eye for beauty and style.

As a sensitive, thoughtful person, I knew my business had to deal with a product or service very close to my heart. As you can tell by now, cats have inspired love in me from the beginning of my life. My cats, Maya and Baby, very quickly made me realize that I wanted to make a difference in our furry friends' lives. So I decided to become a "catpreneur," designing and providing beautiful, eco-friendly furniture and organic bedding for all the felines we love.

A massive quantity of cat-related products is available on the market. Yet, as I dug deeper into what was available, I saw clearly an absence of products that met my high standards of quality and design. Instead, most cat beds I saw were either unattractive or poorly made. I didn't want to give one of these to my babies, nor did I want these ugly beds in my living room.

Also, I could see that cat parents like me were becoming more vocal about honoring the nature of our cats. Cats, after all, are not just small dogs. As such, they have their own unique needs.

Until this point, the cat products available almost seemed to be an afterthought of the pet supply market. This measly supply of products could usually be found hidden away in the back, left corner of pet stores, overshadowed by the larger and more proliferated dog market. Finally, however, more and more companies are beginning to develop innovative products for cats and their cat parents to create a more diversified product portfolio. I didn't just want to be a part of this move-ment toward providing a better array of cat-related products —I wanted to be a pioneer who caters to cats and offers groundbreaking products that are both aesthetically pleasing and environmentally safe.

I started CatsEssentials because I believe modern cats deserve the best—and modern cat ladies (and gents) deserve to have products for their furry babies that are just as beautiful as both they and their cats are.

Early childhood lessons

As a child, I was quite independent. This actually drove Mamma Rosa nuts. She would often say, "Melissa, let me help you with your homework," or "Let me help you pack your suitcase for our trip!" But I never wanted her to help me. I knew I could do things for myself. It's part of my character to prefer to do things on my own and not let someone else tell me what to do or think. I suppose this trait worked well for me in my later years as an entrepreneur.

I was a very particular child. In Italy, the school year starts in mid-September and ends in mid-June, giving us three months of summer vacation. I looked forward to each fall when I would prepare for the upcoming school year, lining up my textbooks, notebooks, and pens. As a left-handed student, I was very particular about my pens. I would make my poor mother spend hours in the bookstore while I tried every single pen they had. Many of them would cause the ink to stain my hands and make a big mess on the paper. Every autumn, my mission as a young girl was to find the perfect pen for me.

Mamma Rosa tells me now that I was always a very neat child. Everything belonged in its place. Again, another trait of mine that I suppose has served me well in my adult life and business. I likely got this trait from my mom, who is spotlessly clean and exceptionally well-organized.

As a child, I spent a lot of time with my Papà Galliano. He could fix or build anything, and his penchant for manual work rubbed off on me. He made his own machines to produce the shoe parts in our factory. Papà didn't just buy a machine—instead, he constructed it from the ground up with his own hands. Papà is basically a self-taught engineer.

I didn't play with dolls like most little girls. Instead, I preferred to spend time with my father in his workshop, watching closely what he was doing or making and trying to figure out how he was doing it. Anytime he needed a hand with something, I wanted to help him. He allowed me to use all the special tools to cut and file and build things. He didn't mind if I used these tools as long as I promised to carefully put each item back in the specific spot where it belonged on the wall rack that he had made, where every single tool had an assigned place so that he could find it when he needed it. Papà Galliano had infinite patience for building and fixing, even with intricate projects with tiny pieces. Thanks to my dad, in my business today, I have the confidence and skill to build things with my hands.

So, from my mother, I learned to keep my life and business neat and organized. And, from my father, I learned to build. These two traits became the basis for my current business venture.

The family business

In providing for his family, my father had moved through several businesses throughout the years. He once had a car wash and even used to deliver milk. He and my mother did whatever was necessary to take care of their three girls. I can imagine it was a pretty heavy load for them. My father, an exceptionally creative person, eventually decided to start a shoe factory. Since they attached it to the back of our new house, my mom was able to work with him in the factory while, at the same time, keeping her eye on us children.

My sisters and I helped in the family business, especially during the long summers and other school breaks. I remember my dad would come in through the door that connected the factory to the house and ask if one or more of us could help. Maybe they would be running late for a delivery or just needed an extra hand for something. In any case, if I was in the middle of my homework or another project, I was sometimes not feeling very happy about it. However, I also understood that it was vital to contribute to the family business and give my parents a hand when they needed it. My dad was always so sweet when he asked us girls to come assist in the factory—almost as if he felt bad asking. So I knew that if he came through that door asking for help, he truly needed it.

What I learned from my parents' entrepreneurship

Throughout the course of watching my parents run their business and live their lives, I have learned so much. However, the most important thing I learned was the true meaning of the word "quality." Both of my parents frequently repeated, "If a piece does not come out perfectly, do not put it in the box. We will redo it or replace it with another piece."

This adherence to quality transferred over from what we produced into what we bought. If I was out shopping with Mamma Rosa, she would always recommend against buying something if it wasn't made well. She'd say it was better to buy one piece of exceptional quality rather than two or three of bad quality since better-made items would last longer. This quality over quantity mentality has stayed with me even to this day.

I also learned a stellar work ethic from my parents, who were highly respected in our community by both their workers and their customers. My parents are very sincere and always try their best at everything they attempt. They taught me to be honest with people, be on time, respect deadlines, and take pride in the quality of my work. They didn't send defective products from their company because it would reflect poorly on them. They also taught me to be nice to people and help out whenever possible. My parents are masters of that. If they are able, they will help anybody who asks. This is why everyone loves them and thinks they are a wonderful couple.

They also gave me excellent time management skills. On one of my recent trips home to Italy, my parents reminded me of how I used to ride my little bike around the factory when I was a kid. I liked to check on the factory operations, and if I noticed that my mom's pieces were running low at her station on the assembly line—I would pedal to my dad and tell him to bring my mom more pieces. This was a small way we avoided time-wasting in our family factory! Even as a young child, I understood that time was money.

In my business today, I also carry over my parents' value of perseverance. When you're running your own business, you will face many challenges. Sometimes, unexpected things happen. Maybe a supplier doesn't deliver on time, causing a delay in the production cycle. Or you might need to deal with an angry customer. When these pitfalls come up, a business owner must always have a Plan B and be ready to quickly find a fix for the problem—even if it is just a temporary Band-Aid until you have time to figure out a longer-lasting solution.

As a business owner, I have found that I must persevere even when facing the inevitable adversities that come my way. I cannot simply give up. Eventually, after sticking to my goals, I will succeed. And I learn from the failures.

Another lesson my parents taught me early on was that I need to work hard if I want to accomplish something. The success fairy will not come and grant me success with a wave of her magical wand. Nobody is going to give me anything for free. I have to work for it. My success is up to me.

My entire essence poured into CatsEssentials

After learning all of these lessons from my parents and getting through my education, it was time to leap into a business I could pour my heart into. So, I created CatsEssentials to offer our feline friends a better and healthier life and to delight cat parents with stylish, functional, and safe products. I do this by providing products that use only natural and organic materials and fabrics to protect our precious environment and to keep our sweet cats safe and healthy. Also, for every wood-designed product purchased from CatsEssentials, we plant a tree in the Amazon rainforest and donate a percentage of all proceeds to no-kill cat shelters.

As a social entrepreneur and modern cat furniture designer, I've made it my mission to reinvent how the world provides quality, comfort, and luxury for our beloved feline companions.

My furniture collection replicates a small-scale version of the high-end furniture sophisticated cat parents commonly enjoy. The products I offer are of the highest quality and are inspired by contemporary Italian furniture. Just as my parents taught me, I don't sacrifice when it comes to excellence.

Our cats are our babies. They are our family, and we want to provide them with nothing but 'the best.' This is why in July 2022, I incorporated a new tagline for my business: "For Spoiled Cats Only."

There's no doubt about it: we cat lovers want to spoil our felines. We have an almost irrational urgency to provide our cats with the ultimate luxurious experience. So luxurious, in fact, that we might even envy our cats their comfortable lives. Some of my customers have actually sent me requests, asking me if I can provide a product for them—in a human size— that is just as wonderful as the furniture I created for the cats!

The bottom line: I wanted to create a product line that represents us, the modern cat ladies. We want our home's items to be of impeccable quality and strike us as aesthetically pleasing. Our beloved feline children deserve this—and so do we!

In my role as a luxury "catpreneur," I am quite vocal about my belief that we are not cat owners but rather cat parents. The human-cat bond is crucial to me, and I believe calling myself the owner of any animal is an insult to the animal and betrays the special bond we have with each other. Although we are obviously not biological parents of our furry babies, our emotional connection with them is so strong that some of us consider them our own children.

I hold my beautiful cats in high regard. They are wonderful sentient beings who deserve respect, love, and good care. I believe it's my mission to be the mom of two happy and healthy cats, and, through my business, I want to help other cat parents do the same with their own feline babies.

6

Is My Cat Happy?

Because my fur babies depend entirely on me, I feel an enormous responsibility to do my best to keep them healthy and happy.

How do we know if our cat is happy? Well, isn't that the million-dollar question of any cat parent? If you're like me, you've decided to keep your cat indoors only, then you must make sure they have a fulfilling life. To me, being a cat mom means stressing about my furry babies.

- *How do they feel?*
- *Are they happy?*
- *Are they experiencing any pain?*
- *What veterinarian should I choose?*
- *Will they be happier if I allow them to go outside?*
- *How do they feel when I'm not home with them?*

Yes, these questions can be overwhelming, and the truth is there are no easy answers. At the end of the day, we are the ones responsible for our furry kids, and we have to make the right choices on their behalf.

Understanding their behavior

Cats may seem untouchable at times, sophisticated to the point of unreachable. However, they experience a myriad of feelings and can communicate these feelings to us. If we are in tune with what our cats are trying to say, we'll be better equipped to take good care of our little fluff balls.

The Internet is packed full of articles, expert studies, and advice blogs that discuss what triggers your cat in both positive and negative ways. If you take the time to learn what is happening inside your cat's head, you'll be a giant step ahead. Not only will you find explanations for their behavior, but you'll also learn how to react to that behavior and strengthen your relationship with your beloved feline.

If we better understand what our cat is doing and why, we can curb negative behaviors like spraying, litter box issues, or aggression. Nipping conduct like this in the bud will keep our households running more smoothly and solve the emotional problems behind our cats acting out.

So much of our cat's health and safety is our responsibility, not our vet's. We cat parents are responsible for our furry babies, and we need to do our best to keep them healthy and happy by being proactive and working to prevent anything terrible from happening to them. The more we learn, the more we are prepared for our job as cat parents.

Spend time watching and listening

Yes, learning about cat behavior from expert sources will go a long way toward making your kitty happy. However, learning is only part of the scenario. Internet research does little good if you aren't taking into account the specific behavior of your own little friend since every cat is unique and shows its feelings in different ways. This is why it is so important to closely monitor your cat and her particular behavior. Try to figure out what she is trying to tell you.

Throughout the years with my furry children, I have learned to read their facial and body expressions, from the most subtle blink of the eyes to every switch of their intelligent tails. I can emotionally connect with them by watching them well; I can feel their mood and emotions. Being aware of their particular language allows me to constantly check in with them to see if they're feeling good or whether something is off. Cats are very good at hiding their pain. However, if we cat parents pay close attention to them, we should be able to see when something is wrong.

Listen to the vocalizations your kitty makes. Your cat will make a wide variety of sounds that will alert you to whether she is hungry, feeling sick or in pain, or even if she just wants to snuggle.

For example, I love hearing Maya's trill when I open the door. She makes this sound to greet me and let me know she's happy I came home. She will also let out a squeak sometimes if I'm not paying enough attention to her or she needs some-thing from me.

Recently, Baby emitted a new deep meow. He looked distressed. After watching him walking around for a few moments, I saw that he was having trouble using the litter box. Poor Baby! He was constipated! Baby will also make a higher-pitched sound when I approach him since he knows cuddles are on the way.

While we may try to categorize these sounds for the purposes of our own human understanding, I believe there isn't a universal language that all cats use. In my experience, my two babies each have very distinct tones and vocalizations. Because every cat is different, it is up to us cat parents to learn how to recognize them and understand what they are trying to say.

Purring is like a language in itself, but unfortunately, we can't reciprocate it with our cats. Despite all of the studies, it is still unclear how this sound is created. Some say that the whole vibration thing begins in our kitty's brain. The purring is not exclusive to domesticated cats. Some big cats purr too—like bobcats, lynxes, and Florida panthers—but, interestingly enough, the ones that roar (like lions and tigers) can't purr. It has to do with the physiological structure of their head's bones and ligaments.

For us cat lovers, the purring is just a wonderful thing! It is another one of those mysterious traits that make our felines so irresistible. The purring pulls us together with our feline companion in an intimate connection. As we pet them, they offer us this magical sound that also has healing powers.

We often connect purring with happiness and contentment, which is true when our kitty lays on us for naps or cuddles. But purring can also be a sign that your cat is stressed or scared. Sometimes cats just purr to heal themselves when they are hurt or injured. Purring is just another example of how magical our cats truly are.

Watching our kitties' body language is another way to discern what is going on behind those mysterious eyes. We cat lovers adore it when our babies blink their eyes slowly at us. We have learned to return this message of love by responding in kind. Also, I know that if Maya is staring at me consistently *without* blinking, she is trying to tell me something. Usually, this means she is ready for a treat!

Often, your cat will find herself in a new situation. For example, there might be a guest in the house, or they hear a new sound. Your cat will look at you to gauge your reaction. She wants to know from you what is going on or how she should respond to this unexpected stimulant.

Baby will seat himself like a little human in the middle of a room when he feels content. He wants everyone to know that he is part of the conversation. He will also happily wag his tail while sitting there, showing his gladness. If, on the other hand, Baby wiggles his tail back and forth in quick, hard movements, that means he wants to play.

While there are a million little clues we can read from our cat's body language, it is critical to learn the ones that indicate our cat is frightened, uncomfortable, or stressed. Signs like dilated pupils, ears pulled back or flattened, or tails wrapped around their bodies might indicate a problem that we humans should pay attention to so we can fix it. Sometimes Baby completely freezes when he is scared of something; other times, he will run and hide in his safe place. While there is some recognizable body language, every cat is unique. Therefore, we should monitor our babies' movements and gestures to better understand them and care for them in the best possible way.

Of course, it was always more difficult for me to have this kind of connection with my outdoor cats. I wasn't this much in tune with those cats since I didn't have the opportunity to spend as much time with them as with Maya and Baby. So, keeping my cats indoors helps me take great care of them.

Help them live life to the fullest

Because my fur babies depend entirely on me, I feel an enormous responsibility to do my best to keep them healthy and happy. When I know that they seem to need something that will make them even happier creatures, I work it into our lives. For instance, Maya and Baby have their own room filled with comfy beds, unlimited toys, water fountains, automatic feeders, and pet cameras. To soothe the cats' moods, Alexa plays soft music from speakers throughout the day. My babies have window perches (to watch the birds outside), scratches, and climbing surfaces. This setting helps a lot when I'm away. Even though I still miss them terribly every time I leave, and I worry that something might happen to them while I'm not home, it is comforting to know that Maya and Baby have everything they might need while I'm gone. Also, the pet camera allows me to keep an eye on them, talk to them, and even play laser tag with them remotely!

Even though they are indoor cats, Maya and Baby have every opportunity to stay active and live a life that is chock full of entertaining and challenging experiences. In their short lives (ten years and nine years, respectively), Maya and Baby have already lived with me in five different homes and traveled extensively. With all the modern travel gear available for cats these days, why not take your feline friend along with you instead of leaving her home or at a boarding facility? Also, I recently started taking them on outdoor adventures, carrying them in a cat backpack. They are learning to walk on a leash, so I can take them outside more often.

Cats need much more than just food and a litter box. It is wrong to assume that they are so independent that they want to be on their own. Instead, they want to live life to the fullest. They need us to give them mental stimulation, daily excitement, and new experiences.

While it's true that cats sleep a lot, they also need our intervention as good parents to keep them active and entertained, or else they will end up sleeping too much and even become apathetic or depressed. Not enough stimulation can also cause our cats to become aggressive or even destructive since their energy needs to be released in some way. It is much better to encourage them to use their energy in positive ways—through play and exploration—than in negative ones.

Let them practice their instincts

A cat is a cat. This means she is her happiest self when she is allowed to act like one. If you see your baby intensely focusing her gaze on something, don't get in her way. She's about to pounce on her next prey, which is something that comes naturally to her. Our little predators are not vicious killers. When they express their hunting instinct, they are merely acting out their lives as true cats, and we need to give them ways to play that suit their instincts.

If your cat lives solely indoors, it's crucial to find a way for her to exercise her urge to climb. Cats are natural climbers—both to pursue their prey and to find safety. There are a variety of climbing trees, towers, and shelves on the market that you can purchase for your cat to climb to her heart's content.

Cats are naturally dynamic creatures, so it's important to provide them with plenty of toys to work out all that excessive energy. Cat toys are fun for your little furry friends. They also stimulate their minds and work out their predatory instincts. It's great for you to get into the mix and play with these toys with your cat, which encourages her to be active and helps you understand her better, and forges a strong bond between the two of you.

Just be sure to choose your cat's toys wisely. They should not have any small, detachable parts that could be ingested while your kitty is playing. Also, purchase toys made from natural or organic materials since your cat will likely be chewing and licking them. Finally, keep toxins and harmful chemicals away from their playtime!

Give your cat the gift of companionship

A cat prefers dedicated one-on-one time with her mama or dad. She wants your full attention zeroed in on her and her alone. This is much better than half-paying attention to her while doing something else.

However, most cat parents have full lives and simply cannot be with their furry baby all day and night. Even if we prefer this, we have many responsibilities outside of our home that take us away. While you are gone, how does your cat stay active? Well, one way to solve this problem is to adopt a friend for your feline—another cat! Of course, this is not a universal solution as it depends on your specific family situation and, most importantly, the temperament of both your cat and that of the new addition. We must respect their individuality and see if the two can be compatible.

But if it's doable, then adopting another cat can be a win-win for you since your first cat gets a friend, and you... well, you get a second kitty to love. Having a furry companion to play with will keep your feline happy and stimulated. We all know that a playful, active cat is a happy cat.

It doesn't take a lot to have a happy cat. Mindfully observing our babies while offering them things to improve their lives will go a long way to our feline's overall happiness. In the next chapter, I'll offer some ways to spoil our cats once we learn what is best for them.

7

How To Spoil Our Cats

Spoiling our cats is about offering little gestures to our beloved sweethearts, like staying put when our cat is nestled into our laps, purring, no matter what you feel you need to do at that moment.

When we use the term "spoiled" when referring to a person, most of us get a bad taste in our mouths. It is often associated with a negative demeanor. However, when it comes to us cat parents, all we want to do is spoil our cat babies. Spoiling is an unavoidable proposition for a cat lover and is usually a sign of how much we love our cats!

After all, we think, *what is the worst thing that could happen if I spoil my fur baby?*

It's okay to spoil our cats

Spoiling our cats is the thing to do. It doesn't ruin them. On the contrary, it only makes them happier. So why wouldn't you want to give your cats the best? Most cat parents I know, myself included, love to pamper our cats and help them enjoy the most lavish lifestyle. It's our way to show our love for them and our appreciation for them as our companions. We're not afraid to shower them with the good life and then share pictures of the same with our fellow cat lovers. This is why the Internet and social media are chock full of images of "spoiled cats" that likely live better than many beings on this planet.

We don't hold it against them

What other creature gets to sleep for hours a day while the rest of us have to go to work? Still, we spoil them. We can't seem to help ourselves. Maybe it's because seeing them lounge sleepily on silk pillows, climb joyfully on elaborate cat towers, and delicately eat their food from fancy dishes makes us proud that we can give them such a good life. Planning a spa day or a birthday party for our kitty gives us a thrill. Buying our cats furniture—like the luxury items I create—makes us happy inside. It's just so much fun to take fantastic care of these gorgeous little critters.

Some cat parents go so far as to give their kitty their own iPad with fish and bird apps—like Friskies CatFishing, which challenges your cat to "catch" fish on the screen. These apps give your cats something to play and watch. This trend of setting an electronic device in front of little Tiger really took off during the Covid lockdown since people found themselves working from home—they wanted their cats to have their own entertainment while they worked from their laptops. Plus, another bonus: if the resident fur ball is occupied with an app, they would be less likely to jump comically into the frame of the Zoom meeting their human is currently conducting.

Often, people will hold the misconception that cats see us as their servants. I totally disagree with that. Our furry babies love and appreciate us. As cat parents, we treat them well. We love and respect them for who they are, and they love and respect us in return.

We invited them into our houses, so that means we have a responsibility to take care of them. After all, if our cats lived outside, they would be capable of catching their own food and would not need a litter box. Feeding our babies and cleaning the litter box shouldn't make us feel like servants—it should feel like an act of love.

What is "spoiling"?

Spoiling our cats is not about simply purchasing the most expensive or fanciest items for them. Instead, it's about offering little gestures to our beloved sweethearts, like staying put when our cat is nestled into our laps, purring, no matter what you feel you need to do at that moment. It's about giving them extra cuddles or a brushing session, making them feel loved and pretty. It's about observing their behavior and giving them what they need when they need it.

Therefore, anything we do to improve their lives, even if that just means showering them with extra attention, can be considered an act of spoiling. Other ways to spoil your baby include:

- Creating a comfy space for them.
- Treating them to an edible garden (with tasty grasses like wheat, barley, oat, and rye).
- Giving them a new toy, maybe one that is filled with a bit of catnip.

- Creating a "catio" for your indoor feline, complete with cat-safe plants, comfy beds, and many perches to climb.
- Taking a nap with your sleepy baby.
- Petting your furry feline frequently throughout the day (this makes them happy and you, as well—research shows that petting your cat for just ten minutes per day helps relieve stress!).
- Choosing a veterinarian with a holistic, natural approach that takes care of many feline patients.

The one way we should NOT spoil our kitties

Yes, you can nuzzle your cats all you want and play with them as much as you can. These things will not spoil your cats. One thing, however, you should not do is spoil them with excess food. Even if your fur baby continuously asks for a meal or snack, you should restrain yourself from giving in. This will only lead to your *Fluffy* becoming *flabby*. She will become lethargic, and her lack of activity can lead to heart disease, hypertension, cancer, or diabetes.

After reading articles and books about cat nutrition so I could take better care of my babies, I learned that a cat's diet should consist of high-quality meat, not the carb-heavy dry food that tends to bring on obesity and possibly diabetes. A healthier, meat-based diet is definitely a little more expensive but is a great way to spoil your cat and help him thrive.

If you want to treat them with food, try to buy the healthiest treats available and use them as positive reinforcement when your babies learn to do something new. You can also put these treats into a puzzle toy to keep them entertained and mentally active.

Offering food is seen as an act of love, but overfeeding has nothing to do with affection. If food is not offered in a healthy way, then the results can be disastrous. Unfortunately, cat obesity is much more common than we think, especially in North America. More than 50% of indoor cats in this country are either overweight or obese, conditions that are detrimental to our pets' health. Our primary concern as cat parents should be to keep our cats physically healthy. Food is the one thing we shouldn't overdo when spoiling our babies.

When we want to spoil our fur children, we can find multiple ways to enrich their lives (and ours). There is no way we can spoil our cats by loving them too much! So don't wait for National Cat Day on October 29. Love your cats in the best way you know how this very day—and spoil away!

8

Cats Are Sentient Beings

Cats have a magical allure that makes us humans feel a deep sense of calm.

Cats are sentient beings, just as we are. What do I mean by that, exactly? According to the Cambridge dictionary, "sentient" means "able to experience feelings." This means that they can perceive and feel things. They have an incredible power of perception and are able to use their senses in a way that many creatures cannot. Also, they are conscious of their environment and the intricacies of the aura around them.

Cats can *feel* things.

Synonyms for "sentient" include: alert, attentive, awake, aware, cognizant, observing, perceiving, noticing, responsive, seeing, feeling, understanding, sensitive to, and watchful.

Our adored felines have a higher connection with spirituality and a deep inner wisdom. Cats are more attuned than many creatures and are known to have healing powers. Perhaps this is one reason we love them so much. But, yes, it is just one of the *many* reasons!

Many would argue that cats' sensitivity is even deeper than that of humans. They can feel our deepest emotions and thoughts, even though we sometimes have a hard time feeling them that same way. If we are feeling unwell or emotionally upset, they seem to know. They will even try to cheer us up with a paw boop or an arm knead.

In light of the loving care our cats give us, the least we can do is attempt to understand what they're trying to tell us. If we can tune in to our cat's frequency, we will find we are communicating with a mammal that is much more than just a cute ball of fur. Opening ourselves up to the cat's energy, we can empathize with them and connect on a deeper level.

Securely attached

A research study published in the journal, *Current Biology*, found that a majority of cats—64% in the study—will securely attach themselves to their humans. This means that they trust that their human will take care of them. For example, a securely-attached feline, if left alone for a little while, will greet her humans when they return and then go back to what she was doing. This proves that she isn't terribly upset by your absence and has faith that you will return to her.

Insecure cats will seem more needy. Signs of insecurity include swishing their tails, biting, hiding, meowing excessively, and even peeing all over the house.

While some might think that cats are standoffish, the cool and collected cat behavior we often witness in these beautiful creatures simply points to a secure feline. Sometimes, we want our cats to display the over-excitement dogs do when greeting their humans. However, as I've argued before, a cat is not a dog. Cats are their own beings.

It's okay that our feline babies love us in their own cat way. They are only expressing themselves as they innately know how. However, it's important to remember that they are definitely more attached to their humans than people sometimes give them credit for.

Spiritual lessons from our feline friends

Cats are natural Zen masters. Eckhart Tolle, spiritual teacher and author, has said, "I have lived with several Zen masters—all of them cats." We can learn so much from our feline friends about how to increase our concentration, eliminate negative energy, and become more peaceful and mindful. They are enchanted creatures who know how to sit still and contemplate the world. They are not lazy—they just know how to rest in the present moment. They sleep when they're tired. They eat when they're hungry. Whether they are sitting and staring into space, napping, or playing, they are utterly in the moment. We humans often forget how to be as mindful as this.

Cats purr at a frequency of 26 Hertz, which is the same frequency used in vibrational therapies that facilitate tissue regeneration. If this is a coincidence, it is an awesome one. I know for a fact that when Maya sits with me and purrs, my stress levels immediately plummet, and my happiness level skyrockets. Cats have a magical allure that makes us humans feel a deep sense of calm.

Aside from their unmitigated mindfulness, cats also have zero ego. Some people will say the opposite—that cats are selfish little creatures who think they are superior. This is just not the case. While they are confident and serene, cats are not full of themselves. Instead, they are beatific, humble, and almost pure soul.

Cats are extraordinarily spiritual. We can learn so much from them. If we follow their pawprints, we will become happier, more self-aware, and overall better human beings. In fact, just sitting and relaxing with them brings on a sense of mindfulness as they almost seem to shift the energy in the room with their purring, their sleepy eyes, and their mysterious charm.

Cats can also be spiritual messengers. By coming into our lives, they have a specific mission that they are trying to accomplish. It could be a lesson that we need to learn, a roadblock that we need to move, or a message that we need to receive. Some cat lovers have reported that their beloved cats visit them even after they have passed on. These cat parents feel their cats act as their guardians and spiritual guides.

Author Penelope Smith asks in her book, *Animals in Spirit: Our Faithful Companions' Transition to the Afterlife*, "Why would an animal come back to the same person? Sometimes it's to continue their mission to help, guide, and serve. Some animal friends feel you can't do without them!"

Cats choose us

Even though cats can easily survive in the wild, they choose to live with humans. This is an amazing fact that delights cat lovers the world over. Their choice to live with us and be our companions proves that cats have an unusual consciousness for a creature in the animal kingdom. Instead, they have a spirit and willpower to make decisions freely.

A University of London research study found that cats are highly autonomous—even more so than humans. This means they're not dependent on others to protect them or make them feel secure, even though they do feel a sense of security with their humans at the helm. That's why it is so special that they *choose* to love us. They don't need us to take care of them. They just want to be our friends. We should cherish the fact that they have chosen to stick by our sides.

Even though cats can sometimes seem aloof, they love us very much. Another study conducted in 2017 found that cats choose to be near their favorite human when eating, playing with toys, or interacting. Our fur babies are quite sensitive to our moods and emotions and understand us much more than we think. Every cat lover knows this intrinsically.

9

Cat Advocacy

To responsibly care for our feline babies, we need to understand the true essence of the feline species.

Cats are too often described as aloof, detached, and untrainable. While some memes that describe cats in this way can give us a chuckle, we cat lovers know that these descriptions can't be farther from the truth. As people who love cats, we should unanimously advocate for them and present them for who they truly are: beautiful, intelligent, loving, affectionate, sentient beings who make our human lives better.

Micetta and TNR

I'd like to tell you a little story about something that happened to me recently. It relates to advocating for cats in the way that they need.

It was late June, just over a year ago, when a small gray tabby showed up in our backyard. This beautiful little cat looked to be about a year old. She had gorgeous tiger-like markings and contrasting dark, light gray, and white socks. She was in good-looking shape. When I first saw her, I assumed she was one of the neighbors' cats.

However, she began to appear more and more often. I noticed she had a little bit of a swollen belly. It wasn't that big, but I wondered if she might be pregnant. It *was* kitten season, after all!

Much to my surprise, I noticed after a few days that she was eating some organic pellets that I'd put out for my flowers. I also noticed that her belly was gone. She must have given birth and now was starving so much that she was eating my plant food. With this discovery, I immediately went inside for some cat food. Of course, this little tabby devoured what I set in front of her. After she had eaten, I began to look around the yard to see if I could locate the babies. Unfortunately, there was no sight of them. Mama cat came back twice a day to be fed, but I could find no trace of her kittens.

After a few weeks, I was given the most beautiful surprise. While I was taking care of the flowers in the garden, the mama cat emerged from some bushes. Right behind her were these tiny, furry creatures—I counted them, one-two-three-four—jumping all over the place. Four little fluff balls happily bopped around next to their serene mother, exploring their exciting new world.

I was so happy to see that these babies were okay and especially delighted that the little mama cat decided to bring them over to our house. What a beautiful sight to see this happy, healthy family of kittens with their mother, who I named Micetta (which means "small female cat" in Italian).

For the next few weeks, the cats entertained me by running around and playing with each other or taking long, peaceful naps in the sunshine. I was filled with joy at the sight. I soon realized they would come to our yard to run and play, but the neighbor's shed was their home base. The yard was suddenly filled with happiness.

Unfortunately, I knew this setting was not the best environment for them as it presented many dangers. Local wildlife was a threat, of course, as was the busy street on the other side of the house. I was very conflicted about what to do. I did not want to see these cute babies snapped up by a big bird or run over by a car. I researched to find a solution, and it became clear that it was best for them to be adopted. They needed me to find each of them a loving home. However, I procrastinated for a while because I did not want to take Micetta's babies away from her.

But time was running out. At this point, the kittens were about ten weeks old—old enough to survive without their mom. Kittens need to be socialized at an early age; otherwise, it becomes more difficult for them to trust humans. I could not keep them since I already had my own two babies at home.

I contacted a local no-kill cat shelter and asked them if they would take the four kittens for adoption. To my surprise, they had room for them. However, they had to do a blood test first to make sure none of them were positive for the feline leukemia virus (FeLV). Nevertheless, it was good news that the shelter had room for these babies.

I gathered my courage, scooped up the four kittens, and brought them into the basement. I made a nice room for them with large dog crates, beds, litter boxes, and food. At first, they were a little confused about the whole thing. *Where is Mom? Who are you? Why are we inside here?* The tiniest and prettiest of the bunch was the most vocal, crying her little heart out for her mama.

After a while, they warmed up to me. The little one—truly a purring machine—started purring whenever she caught sight of me. When she began her humming vibrations, her brothers and sister would follow suit. I loved this, and I loved caring for them. They had come a long way from being born in a shed in someone's backyard. However, even though I really enjoyed watching these little creatures grow, I also experienced a little stress from taking care of so much. Every day, I asked myself, "Am I making the right choice in putting them up for adoption?"

I felt terrible, especially for the mama cat, whose babies I essentially stole away from her. At first, I caught her too and set her in one of the crates with her babies. However, she was desperate to get back outside. She didn't want to be in there, not even to be with her babies. So I had to release her. Unfortunately, all this accomplished was a frantic scene: the mama walking outside, wailing, looking for her babies, and the kittens inside, crying for the mama.

I found myself crying for all of them.

Those first few weeks before the shelter appointment were hard to handle for me. I felt overwhelmed with the responsibility of caring for all these beautiful creatures. I found it so difficult to witness Micetta's pain. I felt somehow that I was going against what I believed in. Cats are independent creatures—their own beings with their own personalities and feelings. Was I hurting them by deciding on their behalf from my (perhaps limited) human point of view? We humans think we know what's best for cats, but maybe we should just let them live their lives in their own way.

Finally, the day of the shelter appointment arrived. I was even more stressed. These four fur balls had finally started trusting me, but I was planning to leave them in a new environment, where they'd be passed on again to some other human strangers. I hoped against hope that they'd be adopted together or at least in pairs.

The blood tests went well. All the kittens turned out to be pretty healthy except for some slight respiratory issues in the two girls.

My heart was broken when I left the shelter, leaving those babies behind. In the short time they had lived with me, they had given me so much love. Upon arriving back at home, I didn't know how to look Micetta in the eye when she showed up, as usual, for her food. I asked for her forgiveness. I knew I had hurt her.

A few days later, I took Micetta to be spayed and vaccinated against rabies—another very stressful experience! I had to trap her the night before. She would not even let me touch her. After the surgery, I kept her inside until I was sure she felt pretty good and the surgery medicine had worn off. As soon as I released her, she seemed like she was doing great and even ate the large plate of food I set out for her. After she took off, I thought I would never see her again.

To this day, every time I think about this story, I get emotional. But hang on… it does have a happy ending. A few weeks later, I heard from the shelter that all the kittens had been adopted, and right before the holiday season, no less! They had been adopted in pairs, just as I had hoped. One family took the two boys, while another family took the two girls. Happy day! This made me feel so good to know that all the kittens now lived in loving homes.

As for Micetta, well, she's still around. In fact, she has become the Queen of the neighborhood. She protects her territory from intruders. I love seeing her sweet face every morning when she sits on my patio, waiting for me to get her breakfast. She recently started making soft, short meows when I open the door. Just a couple of days ago, I was able to gently stroke my finger along her body. She still doesn't let me pet her, but we are getting closer, thanks to my patience, respect, and love.

Micetta has taught me much about life, forgiveness, and independence. I do wonder where she goes to sleep at night. I also worry when I don't see her for dinner or see her roaming around late at night. Still, I must remind myself that this is the life this proud, independent cat has chosen. She has chosen to be free, and I need to respect that.

From this experience, I have come to admire all of the volunteers who help out in cat shelters, not to mention the trap-neuter-return (TNR) groups and foster moms and dads. TNR is indispensable in keeping cats healthy and their colonies under control. In addition, more and more organizations are showing up worldwide to help control cat overpopulation. The work that all these amazing people do takes a lot of compassion and love, along with the ability to detach their feelings for the good of the cats.

I have learned so much from Micetta and her babies, and I am grateful that she showed up the way she did and is still around.

How to be a responsible cat lover

To responsibly care for our feline babies, we need to under-stand the true essence of the feline species. Throughout this book, we have explored the many ways we can keep our indoor cats happy and healthy. But being a responsible cat lover goes way beyond caring for our house pets. It means understanding the feline species deeper so that we can better provide and advocate for them.

It is so important to project a positive image of cats. So many people see cats as detached or superior. You've probably heard of all the negative connotations people use when talking about cats. While there has been a big social switch where cats are becoming increasingly popular as pets, a percentage of our society still doesn't like cats—or will even go so far as to hurt them. I saw that early on as a little girl when my sister found the neglected white cat, Micia.

Cats need our help to protect them from danger, especially human danger.

If we continuously project a positive image of what cats truly are—independent beings acting in their unique cat-like way—perhaps more people will take a liking to this beautiful species. I think a whole lot of misconceptions can be easily changed simply by sharing the right information.

We cat people know how much we love to talk about our cats, so let's prioritize sharing the positive qualities of these amazing creatures and how wonderful our babies make us feel. Of course, you never know if what you say can sway someone who says they don't like cats. Perhaps they just don't understand them. But, when you share your positive stories and anecdotes about cats, you may even be able to persuade someone to choose a cat as a pet.

Cat overpopulation is another huge issue in our world today. Naysayers see this as the cats' fault. Unfortunately, too many cats are still euthanized every year after ending up in cat shelters and not getting adopted. Let's do our best to support the no-kill cat shelters that work hard to find loving homes for unwanted kitties. These shelters never let the cats down.

Most of us have probably come across stray or feral cats. If we feel the need to feed or otherwise help these cats, we just need to make sure we are doing the right thing for them. It's essential to keep the cat overpopulation problem to a minimum. Therefore, when you see feral or stray cats, after making sure they don't belong to anyone, contact a local shelter or other organization that will take care of trapping these cats and spaying or neutering them. After this is done, the cats must be returned to their territory.

If you start feeding stray or feral cats, please make sure it is a continuous effort. Once they begin to count on you and your gifts of food, then you should keep feeding them, or they will go hungry. In desperation, they may start roaming the neighborhood in search of food and can get in trouble with other cats and people. Not surprisingly, some people do not like feral cats.

Another important role we have as cat lovers is to promote policies that protect cats in all aspects, especially in avoiding their killing. Local legislators and animal control agencies can have a significant impact on this. Perhaps you know someone who works in that field, or maybe you have time to start a conversation about it. You never know what can happen. Look at what happened to Dr. Jennifer Conrad with the Paw

Project. What began with her first approaching the Hollywood (California) City Council has developed into a national organization that advocates anti-declawing legislation and has achieved some major wins!

As cat lovers, the best thing we can do for our beloved cats is to take responsibility to protect them all and help them in the best possible way we can. It is our moral duty.

Final Word

We share our daily lives with our fluffy little creatures, our beloved felines. We can't resist their soft toe beans and wet noses. With their strong yet velvety legs, my own babies, Maya and Baby, have crawled not only into my lap but also into my heart, leaving paw prints all over it. My love for them is so deep that I consider them my furry children. I love them unconditionally, talking to them regularly, rearranging my plans around them, and providing for them in the best way I know.

But it is not just I who takes care of them. My feline family takes care of me just as much. They make me feel better when I'm feeling low—for example, funny little Baby lifts my spirits with his silly ways. As for Maya, her wisdom helps me along my human spiritual journey.

Cats are mysterious and perfect just the way they are. They are special souls that we cat lovers appreciate and feel privileged to know and love. More and more people today consider their pets to be their family, which suits cats perfectly.

I have devoted my entire life to improving the lives of cats all over the world. Born into a family of artisans in Northern Italy, I admire beauty and style, which led me to create my business, catering to cats and cat parents who have an eye for luxury and can't help but spoil their babies. The mission and purpose of CatsEssentials is to provide cats with comfort, love, and safety. This is also my personal mission, as I care for my beautiful family of felines, Maya and Baby, along with all those other cats who come and go in my life.

I hope you have enjoyed reading *For the Love of Cats: A Modern Cat Lady's Journey into Cat Parenthood and Entrepreneurship*. If you'd like to connect with me or learn more about my business, please feel free to reach out. My goal in writing this book was to connect with like-minded, cat-loving people who genuinely appreciate the mysterious, loving, beautiful creatures that our feline companions are. We modern cat parents need to stick together, so I would love to hear from you!

Connect with the author:
Melissa@CatsEssentials.com
www.CatsEssentials.com